Dogs with Baggage!

Getting to know your rescue dog

by

Freddie Fenn

(assisted by Rupert Waddington)

Quotations from 'Give a Dog a Home' by Graeme Sims

(published by Headline Publishing Group, 2010)

Copyright

Dedicated to Freddie

a survivor who taught me so much

and

Ryedale Dog Rescue, Yorkshire,

just one of the many amazingly dedicated little organisations up and down the country

What people say about the book...

"I think is fab and very useful ... the Trustees like the fact it's clear and simple to read, it gets the point across and we love the illustrations too. It really is a very useful little book for people considering adopting a Dog with Baggage."

Annette Pemberton, Treasurer, Greyhound Gap

"I fell in love with this book when I first read it and I believe it fills a much needed gap in 'doggie care' books. Many adoptions can go wrong if the prospective parents are unaware of possible problems. This book addresses many of the problems including excellent advice on settling in, which should go a long way to making sure that these dogs are truly in their forever home.

I especially enjoyed the relaxed and friendly style of the writing and think this should be require reading for all dog adopters."

Vivienne Gardner Edwards. CEO, Angels on Wheels (drug addiction and family support)

"Short and very well-written - this book is a guaranteed winner and will be accessible to even the most reluctant reader - if only more books were as concise and engaging as this!"

Sarah Iveson, Exact Editing

The Bones of the Book

The aim of this little book is to help new adopters during the first few weeks

Roughly 350 animals are abandoned every day (RSPCA November 2012)

If you have experience of bringing up a puppy, your second hand dog will be a little different - not worse, just different.

Adoption's a wonderful choice - a very special relationship

Dogs love routine - so change can be very difficult

They don't know that life is about to get a whole lot better

You are the pupil - your dog is the teacher

Be patient - it will take time

If you're not sure - play it safe, ask for help!

Introduction

So, you're thinking about adopting a homeless dog? Maybe you've already chosen one? Fantastic! Or perhaps you've already done it - but now it feels like it's all going wrong? If so, *don't panic*!

The main aim of this little book is to help new adopters during the first few weeks - or sometimes months - with some tips and encouragement. This is the time you spend getting to know each other, building the foundation for the strong relationship you can both share for years to come.

And if adopting isn't for you - it doesn't matter! It's not for everyone, but by *knowing* and *understanding* what it all involves, you can help to spread the word and encourage others to think about adoption. So please keep reading!

We don't cover training in this book. Why? Training an adult dog, especially one with a bad past, can be very different to training a puppy; each dog may need its own special support and expert help. Your local Rescue or local vet can help you find this.

Contents

The option of adoption   9

Second-hand dogs   10

How big is the problem?   11

Puppy vs Adult Dog   12

How do you decide what's right for *you*?

Baggage, good and bad!   15

The Golden Rule   21

And some other useful 'rules':   22

     Don't make a fuss

     Be consistent

     Be patient

Value the *little* things   27

Help!   28

Do's and Don'ts   30

Help me write the next book!   32

Help your local Dog Rescue   33

News Adopter's Diary   34

A heart-warming tale of two tails....   49

About the author   53

The option of adoption

All but the most abused dogs retain an urge to bond with a human...

Dogs really are amazing animals. Whatever cruelty they experience, all but the most abused dogs retain an urge to bond with a human. It's like a flame of hope that is never extinguished. This means that most dogs which end up in rehoming centres *can* be rehabilitated. Yes, they may have a strange fear or habit which you'll have to learn to cope with - but, with the right support, their capacity to love and *enjoy being loved* will re-emerge, maybe stronger than ever.

> *"Rescue dogs, once settled, return love with a passion because they know that they were once lost but now have been found."*

This is what makes adoption such a wonderful choice. You're saving one more dog from being put to sleep; you're giving that animal the security and basic comforts it has maybe never known; and most of all, you are starting a very special relationship - very special indeed.

Second-hand Dogs

We don't normally talk about 'second-hand dogs', but I think it's a really useful description. Here's why.

Not every homeless dog has been abused; not every homeless dog has behavioural problems. *But every homeless dog has a past.* And whether we know about this past or not, it's what influences our early weeks and months with our 'new' dog. So, the dog brings its past baggage with it, good or bad, into our lives. But because it can't talk and tell us about it, we have to guess and work it out ourselves. And this is what this little book is all about - helping *you* to work it all out.

"Do you know, the only thing you can give away in great measure and still have more than you started with is love?"

How big is the problem?

In November 2012, the RSPCA announced that the number of abandoned animals has risen by a staggering 65% in the last five years. This means that roughly 350 are now dumped every single day! And of course, a great many of these are dogs. Yet people keep breeding dogs for profit, and people keep buying them.

It's a problem needing many different solutions - one of which is to encourage more people to think about adopting rather than buying a puppy. However, adopting *can* bring problems and then, for one reason or another, the dog ends up back at the rescue.

So, we need to find ways not just to increase the number of adoptions, but *to make more of them last*. And that means helping prepare people for what to expect from their 'new' dog - hence this little book.

We'll start by looking at the basic difference between acquiring a puppy and adopting an adult dog, a difference which diminishes with each passing month in the dog's life.

Puppy vs Adult Dog

Bringing up a puppy and rehabilitating an adult dog are different experiences. Both can be a mixture of joy and frustration. But if you know what's involved, you'll be prepared and more than capable of coping. Let's think first about puppies...

Puppies are adorable! All of them, big or small. And they all do adorable things. Watch a little puppy on one of its first walks in the big world; it meets an older dog and instinctively turns on its back, exposing its tummy and letting the older dog sniff it. Just one of the seriously cute ways that puppies are pre-programmed to behave!

Another benefit of puppies is that they are blank canvases, ready to learn from you. So, if you bring it up properly you should end up with a sociable and loving animal, well suited to you and your lifestyle.

However - before looking at adult dogs, let's remember one thing - **puppies are only puppies for a few months.** And soon they are just as likely to do revolting 'doggy' things, to chase next door's cat, to raid the kitchen bin - because once grown up they're - well, they're just dogs like any other.

Now, let's think about taking on an adult dog...

By around nine months old, a dog's character is pretty-well formed. It's still a youngster and won't really be fully adult until well into its second year. But the essential dog and its character is all there - and will stay the same for the rest of its life.

Every adult dog has had early experiences that shape its character

Now of course, not every dog passing through a rescue centre has been abused. But every adult dog has had early experiences that shape its character.

They all come with baggage. And because you can't undo that, you must be prepared to *get to know* your dog in the same way you do a treasured new friend - warts 'n' all.

Is this a problem? Not at all. Sure, if you want to try stamping your own personality onto your dog, you should get a puppy. Don't forget, though, that bringing up a puppy can be exhausting and stressful! If, however, you like the idea of *getting to know a dog*, watching how its true character emerges, encouraged by the security and love you give to it, you will share a different kind of relationship. And in some ways it's an even stronger one.

So, if you have had a puppy in the past, adopting a dog will be different - not worse, just different. And if you've never had a dog before, there's nothing to stop you successfully adopting a dog - and being glad you did for the rest of your life!

Baggage - good and bad!

So, what's all this about baggage?

Well, every second-hand dog has it. That's it. That's all you need to know...

OK, there's a little more to it....but it's a simple concept! Let's take a look...

We all carry baggage with us, accumulated life experiences that make us who we are. Often it's the baggage as much as anything else that we grow to love in each other. And it's just the same with dogs. However, there is good baggage and *bad* baggage, and it's helpful to understand the difference.

The dog with 'good' baggage

There are lots of reasons why happy, socialised dogs suddenly find themselves without a home. Perhaps the owner has died or moved into sheltered accommodation. Sometimes a baby comes along and the dog isn't happy. Or a child develops an allergy.

What's important is that if you *do* want to adopt but are worried about behavioural difficulties, a dog with *good baggage* is your best option.

What problems are there? Fortunately very few! First of all, your dog will probably come with loads of information which makes it so much easier to settle it in. You'll already know what it likes, what behaviour to expect, and you can make the transition much easier. But...

...if a dog feels insecure it will display this in any number of different ways.

Put yourself in your dog's shoes for a moment. One moment life is great - the next it's turned upside down. And the poor dog can't possibly understand why. It just discovers one day that it has a new house in a new area, with new people and new routines. **Dogs love routine so this change can be very difficult.**

What does this mean for you? Just that there will be a period of transition when things *may* go wrong - soiling the carpet, chewing furniture, getting over-excited, not behaving according to the detailed biography it came with. If a dog feels insecure it will display this in any number of different ways.

So, if you know its previous routine, try to stick to it if you can. If not, establish your new one - and keep to it! You can read more about this later under 'Be Consistent'. The sooner the dog learns, and can rely on, the new routine, the happier it will become.

What about the dog with 'bad' baggage?

Remember the RSPCA statistics? Many of these dogs ending up on the streets will probably have lived tough lives up to this point. The lucky ones come under the wing of a rescue organisation, and most of these dogs *can* adapt if given a chance. And the rescue people are very good at identifying those few poor souls who are too badly damaged to be safely rehomed.

Q: Surely an abused dog is thankful to be adopted by a loving new owner?

A: Not always, not straightaway. There are many things an abused dog might have experienced, all of which it may think are just a normal part of life; things such as being:

- Beaten, starved, tied up outdoors and ignored for days on end
- Kept in a shed as a breeding machine with no love or interaction

- Tormented and provoked to develop aggression
- Forced to fight other dogs.

They may not expect anything else.

They don't know that life is about to get a whole lot better.

What they *won't* have experienced is the kind of life *you* are now offering. And it will take time for them to adapt. They won't know that people can be kind, gentle and affectionate. They won't know that they will get fed every day without fail. They won't know that being outdoors, with noise, cars, strangers, bicycles, children, other dogs etc can be safe and fun. They won't know that life is about to get a whole lot better. Why should they?

What is fantastic about adopting a dog with a hard past is watching it change into a happier, more content and trusting dog. It may take weeks or even months - but you'll have made it happen!

So, remember:

- Any second-hand dog will be confused by change, even if it's going from abuse to love
- When its routine is broken, it can behave in unexpected ways - but it won't last long
- Rehoming centres are very careful to learn as much as they can about a dog before putting it up for adoption - but sometimes you're starting with no information at all.

Let's now look at some tips to help you ease your second-hand dog into its new life with you. And if you have other family members, share these tips with them too.

The Golden Rule

You are the pupil - *and your dog is the teacher.* Stick to this rule and you won't go far wrong - and for two reasons.

Firstly, your job as a new adopter is not training or discipline; it's simply to keep your dog comfortable and safe and help it to settle in. The 'no' word may be useful, and some very simple rules can help protect your dog from danger. But, apart from little games to help your dog engage and interact, neither of you need the added stress of serious training at this delicate time.

The other reason is particularly relevant for any dog that may have had an abusive past. As Graeme Sims puts it:

> *"The one ingredient that is ever present with people who treat their dogs badly is an overdeveloped blindness towards the needs of the dog they live with."*

And the best way *not* to be blind? Let your dog teach you all about itself. Watch, observe, wonder, reflect, think, ponder, discuss.

There can be lots of little behaviours that seem to make no sense at all. Worse, you're putting in all this love, time and energy - and at first it can seem as if the dog is rejecting it. Don't be put off and certainly don't take it personally! Just step back, observe and learn. The satisfaction when you *do* get through this and feel so comfortable together is truly amazing! It can take days or it can take months - but you'll get there. What's important is that in the meantime you haven't added to your dog's confusion by mishandling your response.

Here are some other really useful 'rules':

1. *Don't make a fuss*

This is really important with dogs of unknown or abusive backgrounds. You've taken in a dog that might be anxious, scared or confused. Your caring instinct makes you want to comfort and reassure it. Of course you do. But *too much too soon* can have the opposite effect! You see, you and the dog don't

You and the dog don't know each other yet.

each other yet. Imagine you were whisked off somewhere unfamiliar by a complete stranger who then doesn't leave you alone! Would you trust that person?

Some dogs can be withdrawn for a few days when they first move into their new home - it's like being depressed. **Experienced re-homers know that the best thing is to keep a quiet, watchful separation.** Let the dog decide when it is ready to take an interest and explore its surroundings. Give it time and space to get over the newness of it all.

EXTRA TIP

There are some simple ways you can interact in the early days without risking unintended trauma, for example - grooming. Graeme Sims is a great fan of grooming as a life-long special interaction you share with your dog.

> *"For a dog that is new to you, too many cuddles too soon are oppressive and even threatening. Grooming sends a message to your dog. And the message reads: Everything is as it is meant to be."*

But you are still both strangers, so go for a softly-softly approach. Try standing or kneeling alongside, not in front of, your dog and avoid eye-contact. This is much less threatening than the well-meant hug and, done sensitively, can be very reassuring. And always respect the dog. If it walks away, it's probably telling you it's had enough - for now.

2. Be consistent - establish a routine

While most dogs love excitement, they hate change!

Unfortunately, rehoming a dog means change - lots of it. So the important thing is to help your dog to cope with this. And this means *routine*, being as consistent as possible.

> *"Routine will speed recovery from any trauma or disturbance the rescue dog may have suffered."*

As soon as the dog can predict what happens next it will begin to feel more settled. But remember, what seems predictable to *you* may not seem so to your dog! Stick to the routine and watch and learn! And be prepared to let the dog set some of the routine too.

3. Be patient

Be prepared for the fact that it may take time!...

...time for your dog to adjust to the initial change of scene; time for you to get to know each other; and time for you to understand the reasons behind any difficult behaviour and to decide how to work with (or ignore) it.

Now, some rescue dogs and their new owners click almost straightaway and begin forming a powerful bond. However it's not unusual for it to take months before you feel you truly know your dog. And sometimes the longer it takes, the closer the relationship - so be patient!

What this really means is that you mustn't get disheartened within a few weeks if problems persist. And expect the unexpected! Dogs can suddenly spring out of a gloom, deciding that life's pretty good after all. Some can even go through a 'second puppyhood'!

Whatever happens, don't expect your 'new' dog to settle in and be trouble-free within just a few days or even weeks. It may take longer. But have faith that *you will get there!* So, to recap:

- Give your dog time to adjust - lots of time
- Learn from your dog - let it show its true character, likes and dislikes, etc
- Try to be as consistent as possible (and that goes for everyone in the household)
- Give yourself plenty of time - don't expect overnight miracles

Nothing. So the more you watch and think, the more you can work out what is going on inside your dog's mind. And as you get to know your dog better you will begin to fill in some of the blanks. Soon you'll catch yourself smiling simply because at last you accurately predicted what it was about to do. That's when you know you're really getting to know each other. But at the start, just be aware that there are reasons for everything - and because your dog can't use words, your job is to work out what they are!

26

Value the little things

Many dog owners make the mistake of demanding unreasonable or unachievable things from their dogs. Don't do this - it just creates stress and unhappiness Instead, as you get to know each other, *learn to value the little things* that happen as you make progress.

Graeme Sims tells a touching story about Jack, a very confused and unhappy dog which he took under his wing. As with all his dogs, Graeme applied his philosophy of love and understanding in trying to help Jack to enjoy a less stressful, happier life.

> *"At last there is an expression of confidence in Jack's eyes - and for me that is a huge reward."*

I think dogs are put on the earth to be happy. They either share many of our human emotions - or they are clever enough to learn about them so that they can get close to us. Our job with second-hand dogs is to *help them achieve this closeness*, and our own happiness comes from sharing the results.

Help!

You don't have to be an overnight expert!

Just because you have a heart big enough to do this wonderful thing and give a dog a second chance, you don't have to be an expert! Help is out there, and if you adopted via a rescue organisation, they should always be your first port of call. Their members usually share a wealth of experience and will always know someone else to ask if they can't offer the solution themselves.

Sometimes it's hard to know if you need help or not. "I'm being patient and giving the dog space - but he's still peeing on the carpet after 6 weeks....." You're not Super-Owner! Everyone has their limits. And, if you're unhappy, your dog will pick up on this and it will all get worse...

If you're not sure, play it safe and ask for help.

You can also find helpful advice in books and websites. And of course you can turn to professional help - trainers, behaviourists and so on, although you do have to select very carefully. These are not strictly regulated professions and there are still some unkind, old-fashioned and even brutal methods being used.

Here's one more great little piece of advice from Graeme Sims, particularly useful once you've made a few acquaintances when out walking:

> *"It's a good idea to ask someone you see often and who has a well-behaved dog what they think you might be doing wrong with yours."*

What good common sense! Just what you need in bucket-loads to help you get to know your dog in the weeks ahead. Along with compassion, patience, some adaptability - and a sense of humour. It's all you need.

DOs and DON'Ts

DO...

- **Create a quiet dog-only space.** Some dogs like those big crates, others simply want a bed they can go to when it all gets too much - away from enthusiastic little children and away from the noisy TV. Remember to provide a water bowl if using a crate.

- **Register your dog with a vet.** After a few days, it can be sensible to take your dog to the vet for a quick check-up and to make sure they have the renewal date for the vaccinations.

- **Start working on recall.** You'll need this well established before you can let your dog off the lead (see Don'ts below). However, don't think of it as training; just remember to use your dog's name whenever it is coming to you, and reward with a gentle stroke or maybe a dry biscuit. And try not to use its name except when it is coming to you or you are calling it.

- **Change its diet SLOWLY.** Ideally start off feeding whatever food it has been eating and then slowly exchange this for your preferred food over several days. If there is any persistent diarrhoea or constipation, consult your vet.

DON'T...

- **Don't' leave your new dog unsupervised with other pets or young children.** Let everyone get used to each other, and don't take any chances until you feel confident.

- **Don't bring everyone round to say 'hi'.** Not at first; let your dog get used to the new house, new smells, sounds and the family before expanding its social life!

- **Don't let it off the lead.** It's usually best not to risk this for several weeks. The time soon passes and in the meantime you can still be working on recall while your dog gets used to you and to the familiar routes you take when out on walks.

- **Don't get angry!** A short, firm 'No!' is enough if the bin is about to be raided or the chops stolen from the kitchen surface. Harsh discipline is NOT the way to establish trust and good behaviour.

Now, you're probably itching to say *'What about....'* Or *'You've forgotten to mention...'*? OK, that's great because we NEED your own top tips for our next book....read on!

Help me write the next book!

Have you got anecdotes about your own experiences with a rescue dog? Are you willing to share these?

As a ghostwriter and publisher, I know that there is a gap in the market for any book which *tells life as it really is*. Sure, we need the expert guides too but these rarely share stories of when things went horribly wrong - and more importantly, how *these* were put right! They also fail to include the many fantastic and original ways that resourceful dog owners find to resolve little problems.

To this end, I hope to publish another book to accompany this one - stories by people like you who have taken the big step and brought a Dog with Baggage into your home.

All you need to do is email to me a copy of your story - don't worry about the writing - I can give it a good work-out if needed. And if you prefer to remain anonymous, that is fine - but of course you are very welcome to supply your name and, if you wish, a digital photograph of your dog as well (please be careful NOT to include photos of people - just the dog).

Please note - I am looking for short anecdotes. Ideally, choose one behaviour or problem and explain how you overcame it. This type of information will be invaluable to new adopter. Thank you.

rupert@waddington.org.uk

▌*Help your local Dog Rescue*

All profits from the sale of this book are going directly to Dog Rescue organisations (at the time of writing, the proceeds will be split equally between Ryedale Dog Rescue, The Retired Greyhound Trust and Greyhound Gap).

However - there's another way it can help rescue groups - and YOU can help this to happen!

Why not approach your local dog rescue organisation, show them the book and explain that I am happy for them to order copies *at cost* - I can set this up for them and even research the lowest printing options too. They can then sell these for a small profit and/or give them away to new adopters to help reduce the number of failed adoptions.

Please make sure you discuss this fully with the organisation first, and then simply drop me an email to get the ball rolling:

rupert@waddington.org.uk

Thank you!

New Adopter's Diary

Are you a new adopter? If so, it's a great idea to keep some notes of how things are going. This will help you to observe and understand your 'new' dog. But it will also be a wonderful record of the superb work you will be doing as you settle the dog into its new home. Anything that encourages you, giving you cheer when things seem to be going wrong, is helpful!

The next 14 pages are very simply headed and left empty for you to use as best suits you. If you are interested in helping me with the next book (see the previous section) then this record should be invaluable! But even if not, in the months and years to come it will be a marker of just how far you will have come with the dog who, whether bringing good or bad baggage with it, will soon be at the heart of your family.

Week 1

Week 1 continued

Week 2

Week 2 continued

Week 3

Week 4

Week 4 continued

Month 2

Month 2 continued

Month 3

Month 4

Month 4 continued

A heart-warming tale of Two Tails

Sarah Iveson, just one of many hundreds of dog adopters, shares the stories of two adoptions which changed her life.

"My first ever dog was adopted from the Dogs Trust, and she turned out to be the easiest, most fantastic dog you could imagine. She was a lurcher called Twiggy and had been picked up as a stray after being hit by a car. Starving and injured, it was very clear that she had known a cruel hand. In the rescue kennels she was constantly overlooked; not just grubby and covered in scabs, she was also withdrawn and seemed lifeless. That was enough for me - I took her home and will be eternally grateful that I did.

After a while, Twiggy grew into the sweetest dog, making it easy to forget the stress of the first few weeks! She had lots of accidents in the house and, given just a split-second's opportunity, would raid bins or destroy papers. Out on walks she barked wildly at other dogs, and would just about pull me over if she spotted a squirrel or a rabbit. I was totally unprepared! I also had no idea how frightened she would be of
men. It took months for my boyfriend to win her trust, and every time we saw a man while out walking her look of absolute terror was heart-breaking. She did eventually grow less nervous,
but it took a long, long time.

To cut a long story short I eventually learned about her ways and how to deal with it all. The toilet training progressed well and we were soon accident free. Her sweet personality, quirky ways and faultless gentle nature made her a legend amongst family and friends. Even my aunt, normally terrified of dogs, loved Twiggy to bits. Then, after only seven blissful years, she died of bone cancer. Her vet, who had known her the whole time she was with me, cried his eyes out when he came to the house to put her to sleep. He still says Twiggy was the most special dog he's ever known in his whole career.

It scares me to think how easily I could have passed her over at the kennels, not given her this chance - and myself missed out on truly wonderful years of her company.

*

Anyone who has loved and lost a dog knows the routine - at first, total grief and declarations that there can be no more dogs - and then, somehow, another dog comes into your life. This is how it happened for Sarah.

Despite my grief at losing my beloved Twiggy, two weeks after her death I blithely trotted back to the Dogs Trust and said 'give me the dog no-one else wants'. I came home with Solo - a 3-year old Saluki-cross who had been with them for over 2 years!

He was handed in by his female owner, who had had him since a puppy, because her boyfriend was abusing him. Whatever trauma he had suffered was then compounded by being in kennels; he bears the scars of several wounds, some from dogs that he had to share a kennel with. He had twice taken by families but was returned each time when they found they couldn't handle him.

Solo is still with me. It has been a long journey, but one I will never regret. He arrived as a fully grown dog who had never had chance to be a puppy. He went through my house like a tornado, and after the tranquility of living with Twiggy, I didn't know what had hit me! By the end of day one I was at my wit's end, and a jibbering, crying wreck by the end of the first week! Part of his problem was boundless energy - but being far too nervous to go for walks where he could use it up. He refused to go past the end of the drive, and even if I managed to get him into the car, I couldn't get him out of it at the park or the woods, or even once we were back home. So, he took all his energy out on the house.

My family were all telling me to take him back, but I just couldn't - partly because I knew he would never be rehomed again, and partly because I'm very stubborn! I kept thinking what I would
have missed out on if I hadn't given Twiggy a chance. Eventually after about three months, we both began to feel more comfortable with each other. Having bonded with me very strongly, he was starting to take notice of my 'requests'. But it was probably six months before he really settled in and stopped panicking at every small change.

And now here we are, sixteen months after Solo arrived. Things are by no means 'perfect' (for example, when scared he still responds defensively with aggression - he probably always will so it is something I have learned to work around), but you just wouldn't recognise in him the chaotic and terrified dog that first arrived. He is such a character and a really loving dog.

I realise that in a way Twiggy and Solo are opposite extremes, but the bottom line is the same for them both -

if I hadn't given them a chance and found inside myself the patience and capacity to adapt, I would have missed out on so much joy and such incredible relationships. Mind you, I am pig-headed and stubborn! It may not be everyone's cup of tea but if it's yours, then with the right approach and, if needed, support, there is always light at the end of the tunnel."

*

If you enjoyed this short story, you will LOVE the full length story by Tracey Ison, For the Love of Hounds! At the time of writing, her book is still going through the final publishing stages, but if you 'google' the author's name and the title you should find it.

Tracey is a veterinary nurse and brings both wisdom and knowledge to her writing. And the book is an absolute MUST for lovers of whippets and other 'pointy dogs'!

About the author

Freddie (and) Fenn are actually two fantastic dogs (see p1) who inspired the real author, Rupert Waddington.

Rupert is a professional writer and editor - and an amateur dog enthusiast. He knows that good dog management, essential when rehabilitating a homeless dog, is a blend of experience, wisdom, luck, common sense, compassion - and love. And whilst he would never pretend to be any kind of expert, he has had the good fortune to spend many years with a succession of rescue dogs. In a way they have taught him more than any book can - to learn from the dog itself. And his dogs have taught him how to be - or try to be - a better person.

During his experiences with dog rescue organisations, Rupert has met many wonderful, resourceful and patient people but he has also realised that, such is the huge challenge of rescuing dogs, finding temporary 'digs' and eventually a 'forever home', these extraordinary people simply don't have the luxury of time to share much of their wisdom. Longer term, Rupert hopes to create a book which compiles the very best, most sensible and practical as well as affectionate tips from these rescuers and from the many hundreds of adopters of second-hand dogs (interested? See p32). Until then, this little book will hopefully plug a small but vital gap in what is readily available to help new adopters settle in their new dogs.

When not doing or thinking doggie things, Rupert is busy helping businesses and entrepreneurs to create fantastic written materials - eBooks, books, blogs etc.

If you enjoyed this book AND/OR have some helpful suggestions, please contact the author via his website: **www.texteffect.co.uk**.

Printed in Great Britain
by Amazon.co.uk, Ltd.,
Marston Gate.